# SOCIAL SKILLS ACTIVITIES FOR TEENS AGES 13-16

A Guide to Managing Shyness, Making New Friends, Improving Communication Skills and Building Relationships.

By

**J. Schmidt**

**Climax Publishers**

## About the Author

An anthropologist by day, a Sociologist by night. J. Schmidt has written numerous blockbuster books in a span of about 15 years of her writing career. She is well-renowned in educational institutions, especially public universities for her publications regarding sociological aspects of current society. She has also been actively involved in community work and conducting social experiments to raise awareness and providing remedies for today's youth regarding social and cultural aspects. As a mother of two teens, she has devoted much of her life to writing sincere, authentic, in-depth, and to-the-point information. Her books are addressed to both parents and young readers. The knowledge in her books not only stems from her fieldwork and professional side but also from her personal life as a daughter, mother, wife and a, woman.

# Contents

# Foreword

Human beings, like many other living things in the world, have been gifted the affinity of being social with each other and even with other living beings in our world. The book discusses just that; communication and socialization of humans, for not adult humans but rather mini versions of them; teenagers. What drives humans to be social? The core principle lies in interaction and connection. I believe one cannot understand socialization without understanding the root concepts of how socialization develops and works in the world.

For teenagers of the modern era, socialization is quite different than it was back in the day for us many years ago. Today's teens are more "online socials" than "traditional socials," which is fine considering the world technological transitions. Each generation will move through the world according to trends and cultural development. At the same time, the internet provides tons of socialization and communication opportunities to a person from across the globe with considerable safety and security. It does have some drawbacks. Online socialization does not provide the necessary grooming and personality polishing effects, as traditional socialization does.

This book discusses many topics regarding socialization and communication, from basics and fundamental information to modern-day trends, problems and their solutions. This is a comprehensive handbook for teens that offers many exciting, fun, somewhat challenging, and, most importantly, rewarding activities and exercises. The mission of this book is to provide its readers with essential knowledge, especially teenage readers, regarding social skills developing activities; what they are, how they are done, why they should be done etc. and give opportunities to anxious teens and otherwise to develop their social lives in their prime development years.

*So, I wish you happy reading and the best wishes for your teenage years, kids!*

## Message to the Parents

It is a blissful time for couples when they hold their newborn for the first time after birth: a moment of peace and fulfillment a parent never forgets when they first lay eyes on their child.

We devote our minds, souls, and bodies to our child for the rest of our lives, willingly accepting all the consequences, struggles and commitment that come along with being a full-time parent, and it is that very parental instinct that makes us love our children throughout our life no matter what age they become. We not only care for them in their young developing years but also nurture them to be good humans ready for this unpredictable and dynamic world.

Then comes a time in every parent's life when the cute little baby grows up to half your size, starts to annoy you, puts you in a state of frustration and makes you question your life choice of being a parent every now and then. Welcome to your kid's "Teenage Years." Yes, we have all been there! No shame in accepting the feeling of not wanting to be a parent for a moment! But as good parents, we still shrug it off; our personal feelings are thrown aside, and we try our very best to cater to our kids as much as we can; through compromise, sacrifice and tolerance, especially in their adolescent years.

### *Your kid is now a teenager!*

This is a time of great importance, not just for you but for your child as your teenager is navigating physiological, biological and overall emotional and mental changes in themselves and adjusting to the world. This transitioning period from childhood to adulthood is a slightly tricky time for them. I am sure we can all understand because we went through the same many years ago. So, I insist parents to remember their own teenage years, connect with their self from the past and develop a sense of understanding, compassion, sympathy and trust with their teenager. They might lash out at you sometimes, talk back, have negative emotions, and show arrogance or disobedience, but I promise they do not intend on it.

Parents must realize that this is a very unpredictable time of their parenthood. They must balance the freedom and restrictions. Do not be too strict, and do not be too freedom-giving. Teens are also going through differences in their social lives which they have difficulty juggling while making so many other decisions and life choices. During this, many teens become socially reserved and isolated and prefer solitude leading to anxiety and being anti-social. Do not worry; this book will help them develop social skills in an easy, and conventional way while keeping their teenage experience intact. The book is written specifically for teens to read, but parents can give it a thorough reading too to get an understanding of how you can assist your teenage kid in their social development. I encourage you to convince your teenagers to read this book and apply the information provided in their lives. They will understand you and themselves better.

## A Word of Advice for the Fledglings

Hello to my young readers! First of all, I offer you congratulations on becoming an adult, or at least you think that you have become an adult since you are still not off the legal age yet.

I know how you teenagers feel right now. Trust me; I went through the same thing when I was your age. So, I know how you feel on many levels. I like to always call the teenage years a double-edged sword, a phase of your life that can have lasting effects that get rooted into your adulthood permanently. Make good choices for yourself or else making bad decisions in these years will not only affect you accordingly, but will also affect the people who care about you.

I hope my teen readers are better than that or will improve themselves after reading this book. As a teen, your social life is one of the most important things right now. While some teens would prefer to be isolated and away from any kind of interaction or social gathering, others will want to party all night and hang out all day. Some teens are naturally more social, and many become anti-social. This is, of course, all natural. In order to create good social skills in you, I have written this book. The question in your mind may be; Why should I read this book? Why go through a book when I can learn this online? You are right, to some extent. You may learn a lot from various online sources, but what is it that makes this book different from most online sources? Personal experience. I wrote this book out of great devotion from my professional knowledge as well as my personal experiences, both when I was a teenager and formerly as a parent of twin teens.

Did a question mark hover over your head when I called you fledglings in the title? For those of you who are unfamiliar, fledglings are young bird babies that leave the nests after growing fully and strong enough to fly and live on their own. You, youngsters, in many ways can be symbolized as fledglings too. You are leaving a totally dependent stage of life and heading into a life of your own making; choices, plans, decisions, maturity, goals etc., but even fledglings need parting advice and training from their parents or guardians. Thus, my dear teens, it is imperative you have well-developed social and communication abilities since these will be the most influencing part of your personality forever. The bonds you make or break in this age will define you in many ways as a person in the future.

Another thing I want to advise teens before getting into this book formally is to have patience with people who are trying to help you. Yes! I mean specifically your parents and guardians. Please try to understand that we are all here for you and to listen to you, so do not get annoyed by people so quickly; cool down and take a moment to relax and do not hesitate to share your struggle with your loved ones. We went through the same struggles as you when we were your age, so I understand how you think and feel currently. This book is a great socialization kick-start for teens without or with teen social anxiety.

# Chapter 1:
## Fundamental Insights

The first chapter of this book is all about basic ideas, philosophies and scientific facts that will give a preview of things to learn ahead. In order to understand how a particular system works, one must be familiar with what it is for, who it is meant to serve, and what are the requirements and necessities to drive it. The main context of this chapter is to convey an authentic, up-to-date message to the readers about current norms and trends of socialization and communication. Each subsection has a topic of its own and delivers knowledge that will sincerely help you when doing the activities further in the book.

### 1.1 Understanding Interaction & Connection

The word has two parts; inter, meaning among or between and action meaning to act or make a gesture. Collectively it can be summed up as a confrontation or link between two or more individuals as a means to have an effective exchange of messages or information. Interaction is the principle of socialization and communication and the first or initial step, which over time, develops a connection.

Connection is the consequence of repeated interactions. Connecting with people is what builds a person's social standing and charisma in society. Connection leads to understanding, which gives people a sense of deeper understanding and puts things into perspective. Both factors stated above have been introduced from a neutral point of view. It depends on the person that what effect they take or make on interaction and connection in a social circle; it can be either negative or positive.

### 1.2 Factors Driving Interaction & Connection

What is it that drives humans to want to interact? What stimulates humans to be social?

Many theories have existed to answer this. Scientific facts, medical reasons such as psychological need or, in the case of an artistic point of view, a nourishment for the soul, something that fuels desires. Many people have their own answers to the statement; humans are social beings.

What I think is that it is the innate instinct of curiosity to be heard, to feel concluded, to feel wanted, and to want someone. These are some of the many things in humans that run their imagination and spirit to socialize and communicate with those around them.

Humans are one of the creations of Nature. Hence, they are created from the point of positivity and goodness. Loneliness, or being anti-social, the opposite of socialization, has the affinity to kill the inner light and positive energy of the human spirit. So, to my dear teens, I wish and hope that you will try to be as positively social as you can with people.

### 1.3 Socialization & Communication: A Deeper, Honest Look

Communication and socialization refer to a person's awareness of and capacity to comprehend the intentions of others and to express their own intentions in a meaningful and appropriate manner through meaningful and appropriate interaction with other individuals in their environment. Communication and socialization require a person to be aware of and have the ability to do both of these things.

### 1.4 Social Skills in the World

Learning to interact with others is a procedure that starts soon after birth. The years between birth and the age of eight are when people make the most significant social connections. During this time, we also learn the rudiments of our native tongue and

way of life. In addition, a large part of who we become is shaped throughout this time.

Yet, we keep on getting socialized at various points throughout our lives. As we get older, we move into different social categories and must adapt our behaviors accordingly. As we go through life, we encounter lessons that might shape our outlook, values, and character.

There are different types of socialization in the world;

- Primary socialization,
- Anticipatory socialization,
- Developmental socialization and
- Re-socialization.

## 1.5 Current Climate of Socialization Globally

In this digital age, digital communication and socialization combined with cultural and individual mindset bring rapid changes to both the individuals and the society. The current status of socialization and communication in the world is much bland than it was back in the old times, in my opinion. Social media and various online platforms do give an opportunity to teens to socialize and communicate with loved ones and that too from the farthest reaches of the world, but it does not give the development and grooming benefits as traditional socialization used to.

## 1.6 Understanding the Teenage State of Mind

The notion that the brain of a teenager is still developing and going through changes does not in any way imply that it is subpar, according to the latest research. Educators have the ability to foster environments in which students can explore and experiment while avoiding behavior patterns deleterious to themselves and others as a result of the capacity for learning that exists at this age, taste for exploration and the testing of limits. The brain of an adolescent has a greater capacity for plasticity, making it more susceptible to being molded by one's experiences; furthermore, these encounters have a more significant influence than was previously believed. The middle school years present us, as educators, with a number of possibilities that come along only once in a lifetime.

Anxiety and unhappiness in adolescence are characterized by feelings of exasperation, defiance, and a generally pessimistic perspective on life. The adolescent years are a time in the life of your child when they initiate to move beyond the innocent behaviors of childhood and begin testing the limitations and bounds of their development as they get closer to maturity. When limitations and boundaries are disregarded, this can be a source of disappointment for adolescents, which can contribute to feelings of anguish. As a result of the fact that neurological development is not considered to be finished until the age of 24, adolescents have a strong desire for autonomy and independence, but they lack the ability to comprehend or anticipate the various obligations that come along with it.

## 1.7 Social Anxiety in Teens: A Crucial Discussion

One out of every three adolescents between the ages of 13 and 18 years old suffers from social anxiety disorder (SAD). There are currently about 19 million individuals in the United States who battle with a social anxiety disorder (SAD). It is the most prevalent kind of anxiety disorder as well as the third most prevalent form of mental illness in the country. The fear of public interaction and/or situations in which one can feel embarrassed is a defining characteristic of social anxiety disorder, which is often referred to as a social phobia. This fear is ongoing and pervasive. Individuals who suffer from social anxiety disorder experience overwhelming sensations of self-consciousness, anguish, and fear of judgment, even in everyday social interactions. At the same time, it is normal to feel some anxiety in unfamiliar social situations. Those who suffer from social anxiety disorder experience these feelings to an extreme. Individuals suffering from SAD are prevented from having regular connections and interactions with other people. It may also interfere with routine day-to-day activities. In addition, people who struggle with the seasonal affective disorder frequently experience acute anxiety around forthcoming social settings (causing distress days or even weeks in advance).

As a parent, if you see your adolescent having difficulty interacting with others, it's possible they're dealing with social anxiety disorder. Identifying the symptoms of your teen's mental health condition is the first step in getting them the care they need. Following are the manifestations of social anxiety in teens:

- Anxiety or shyness when interacting with others
- Humiliation is brought on through social interaction.
- Insecurity over public ridicule.
- Critical thinking and self-criticism following social interactions.
- Anxiety over other people's opinions.
- Stress out over several weeks or days before a big appearance.
- Aversion to participating in public activities or interacting with other people.
- Problems socializing and keeping connections going.
- Feeling uncomfortable in social circumstances due to blushing, sweating, trembling, or a racing heart.
- Feeling sick to one's stomach or queasy when around other individuals (other physical symptoms may include – confusion, diarrhea, and muscle tension).

There is a universal set of signs shared by all teenagers who suffer from social anxiety disorder (or the same severity). Social anxiety disorder is curable, despite the severity of its symptoms and the many ways in which it can hinder daily life.

## 1.8 Impact of Social Media on Social Interactions of Teens

The University College London study followed 13,000 teenagers for three years, beginning when they were 13 years old, and analyzing how they used social media. The teens also filled out questionnaires regarding their own feelings and well-being, as well as their experiences of interactions on social media.

The study drew three main conclusions after analyzing the collected data about the impact of social media on today's youth:

- Teens didn't get enough sleep since they were up late checking their social media accounts.

- Being cyberbullied or having false or embarrassing information posted online about them.

- Teens sit for extended periods of time without moving around because they spend so much time scrolling through social media on their smartphones and other devices. Therefore, they failed to reap the psychological benefits of regular physical activity.

It became the principal source of social interaction for many preteens and adolescents who, for other reasons, struggled to interact with their pals. According to Halpern, young people can get a variety of benefits from using social media, including "all of which can be powerful, amusing, and social." These are the following:

- Developing relationships with people who share one's passions and interests.

- Increasing one's knowledge in many fields and interests.

- Developing one's identity.

- Increasing participation in social and political activities.

- Getting to know other people.

# Chapter 2:

## Only You Know Yourself

Many great philosophers, ideologists, artists and even some scientists have constantly urged the world to realize the importance of the "self". What is the self? Is it merely knowing your name? Is it just knowing your community? Is it just knowing your daily routine? These questions are indeed a part of a person's self, but this only makes a fraction of this concept. The realization of self is far more grandeur and deep. According to a basic explanation, the self can be said as the part of a person that sets them apart from others, especially when they are thinking about it or acting on it reflexively.

The phenomenon of knowing yourself is quite simple yet complex at the same time. I aim to explain it as easily as I can. Today's society can be quite judgmental and influenced in terms of assessing a person but do not let that get to you. How one knows who they are? There is no answer.

Since that person is the answer, Yes! so my young readers, it is extremely vital for you to know who you are as a person, what you love and hate, what you can contribute and take, what your strengths and weaknesses are, and so many more factors. For a person to know themselves truly and fully is a very important tool in building their personality. How can you communicate with another human being if you do not recognize your own humanity first? So, you see, this concept acts as a pivotal catalyst in a teen's social life.

This chapter discusses some important and basic factors which can help or at least guide a teen to the correct track of how to know their true self.

## 2.1 Principles: The Starting Key to Being Social

A principle can be thought of as a basic truth or idea that forms the basis for a set of beliefs or ways of acting or for a line of reasoning. Principles can be viewed as universal constants; these are essentially lessons and tips that are given to help you combat and manage different kinds of situations in life. The thing about principles is that you can learn or feel them on your own, or someone can educate you about them. Either way, in both cases, these lessons are crucial as they tremendously help in us adult life. Some of the most common and lifelong principles include;

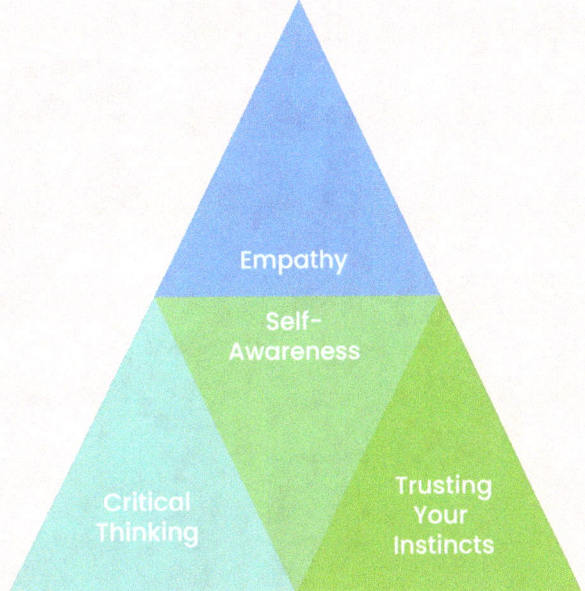

## 2.2 Intelligence from Emotions: How It Helps?

Up till now, you thought that intelligence is a thing of the brain. Some of you may be surprised to learn that our emotions also emanate intelligence. Emotional intelligence actually starts in your teenage and persists throughout your life. The capacity to recognize, name, and control one's emotional responses are emotional intelligence.

During the teenage years, emotions take an initial start at development, and because of that, it can be a little unsteady, but with proper grooming, self-control, and patience, you can easily channel great emotional intelligence by your twenties.

Emotional intelligence is a key factor in a teen's social development since more than half of socialization and communication take their roots from emotions. So, teens should acknowledge the existence and significance of emotional intelligence. As previously stated, it will not be developed right away. It may take some time till you become an adult. However, being more social and doing social activities will enhance your emotional intelligence.

## 2.3 Stop Putting Brakes!

*Societal pressure and procrastination are the two concepts that will be focused on in this subsection.*

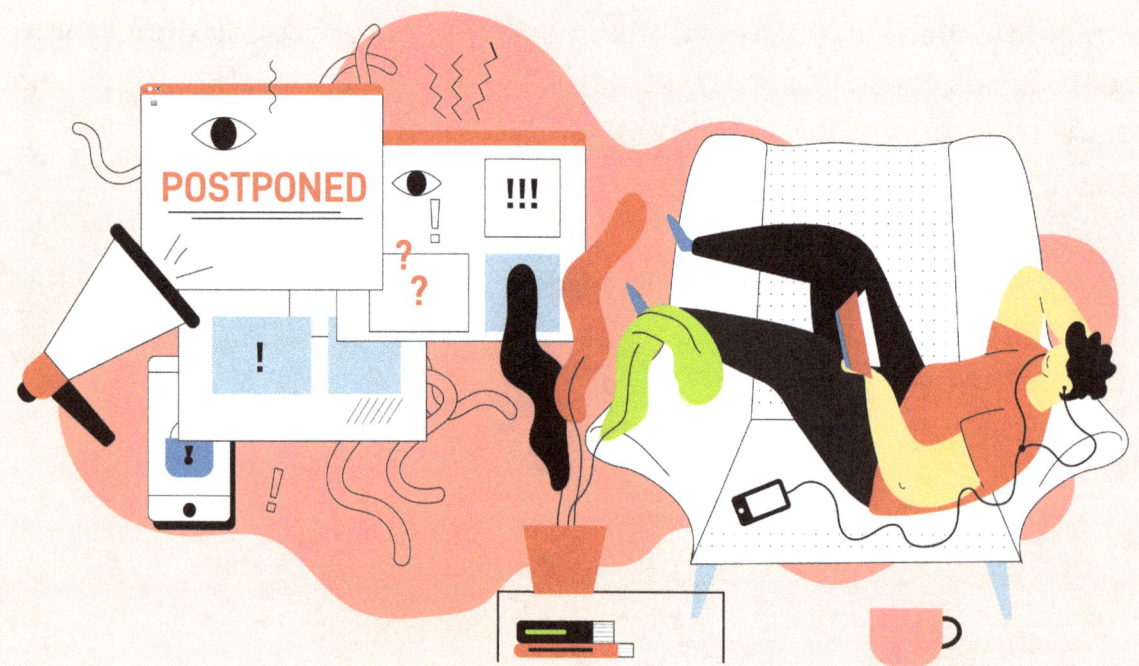

Putting off doing something that needs to be done in favor of doing something that is more fun or easier is a classic explanation of procrastination. The unwillingness to take action characterizes laziness, which is different from procrastination. Constantly putting things off can limit your accomplishments and damage your social and professional development. Procrastination has become alarmingly common particularly in today's youth, because of hectic school and work routines, intense competition, and somewhat unrealistic expectations.

Humans today find an escape, consciously or unconsciously, in procrastination to ease from all the stress and anxiety. For teens, it must be known that procrastination is the enemy of punctuality. Punctuality is necessary not only for professional life but also in your socialization; meet up on time, respond quickly, and reply efficiently etc. So, in order to have good social skills, teens with a habit of procrastination should refrain from it and do give utmost priority to their present task.

Societal pressure is constant social pressure on how we should act, what we should do, what we should dress, and countless other aspects of our life. This pressure occurs all around us and has the potential to influence both the decisions we make and the way in which we make those decisions. It is also able to influence the manner in which we create our distinct identities and determines whether or not we value our individuality. Like procrastination, this, too, is unfortunately fairly common, especially in developing countries and a few parts of rare developed countries. Wherever it goes, its consequence is all the same. Societal pressure does not only come from outside a person's home. Their own family may also subject them to expectations that are a norm or custom in their society. Societal pressure, if given too much, in excess, without rationality, may spew negativity into youngsters' health.

One such consequence is the destruction of self-esteem or confidence. Some teens welcome and accept living their lives the traditional way, which is good. One should respect their roots, but, what about teens who think or feel differently and have a unique view of themselves and life? What if these teens wish to live life and experience outside a traditional view or barrier of society?

For teens with a unique emotional health and mindset, it is imperative that they practice more social activities with people they are very close to and have trust on; starting small is good. The activities in this book can help teens get over the effects of social pressure. So, stop putting brakes on your decisions and emotions due to procrastination and societal pressure, as they will ultimately affect your socialization and communication in the long run.

## 2.4 Charisma

The ability to captivate and sway the attention of others is a hallmark of charisma. Charismatic people stand out from the crowd. However, it is generally much more difficult to specify which abilities or qualities certain people possess that others, less charismatic individuals, do not.

Various traits of charismatic people further complicate the matters. Some people may not speak up as much, and instead depend on their natural charisma to win people over. Still, others have a gift for persuasion and can get anyone excited about anything they're talking about. Charismatic people have developed strong verbal and interpersonal skills. Therefore, charm is a skill that can be honed and enhanced.

Some studies suggest that charisma can be thought of as comprised of a mixture of two factors;

- Amiability-affinity: to be open, accepting and friendly.
- Effect-ability: to take charge and lead.

Develop your skills as a musician, athlete, or student. Some people will be stunned by that, while others will appreciate you. There is no school of thought that can teach you to be charismatic; it is innate but can be somewhat adapted and polished. Even more valuable than charisma is the respect of one's peers, and while leadership ability is innate, it can be developed through practice and experience.

Having charisma is very important for a teen's social life. It shapes a teen's personality to be carried into adulthood. I also had quite a journey forming my charisma during my teen life, it is not something you can achieve in day. It took almost a year building my charisma and social aura and it was worth it. Why? Because I did it with patience, devotion and keen observation skills and these same abilities I will recommend to my teen readers. Fortunately, the many activities in this book will most certainly help you in building charisma and work better on existing great qualities in you.

## 2.5 Final Touches

The core aim of this chapter was to make teens realize some vital prerequisites and startup points before getting into social activities. By understanding the core concepts of principles/life lessons, emotional intelligence, procrastination/social pressure and charisma, a teen can get an idea of the road ahead and the essence of the journey for their good social skills development.

It is natural if some of the concepts stated above skip a teen reader's mind, but do not hesitate to consult your parents and guardians in this matter. Have them read this chapter, so they can clear your confusions regarding the subject of this chapter because it is imperative for teens to understand or realize the essence of this chapter before delving into social skills-building activities in the final chapters.

At the end of this chapter, I want to tell you about my life as a teen when I was 15, I struggled with socialization and confidence too. I had stress from school, from the part time job I was doing and of course, combined with the biological shift. I was shy, did not want to communicate much or interact extra or unnecessarily with people. Some of my teen readers might be in the same situation right now but, trust me, with people in your life, your parents, elder cousins and much help from good knowledge and books, you can overcome these difficult changing times.

# Chapter 3

## Lasswell's Model of Communication

The Lasswell model of communication is a segmented linear framework for describing the process of communication. He suggested that media propaganda serves the following societal purposes: monitoring, correlation, and transmission. For Lasswell, the media has the power to shape how its audience interpret the events.

Developed in 1948 by Harold Lasswell, an American psychologist and sociologist. His model describes the flow of communication in terms of five essential components, each discussed in the subsections below.

If you read about this communication model online or via other academic sources, you will see it is used chiefly in terms of describing how information flows through society using digital media or technological components. While you may think this chapter is unnecessary, the main concept from this chapter cannot be dismissed as it basically gives an overall fundamental understanding of communication in general. For teens, it is vital to understand communication, so this model and its concepts will give you a good idea of it.

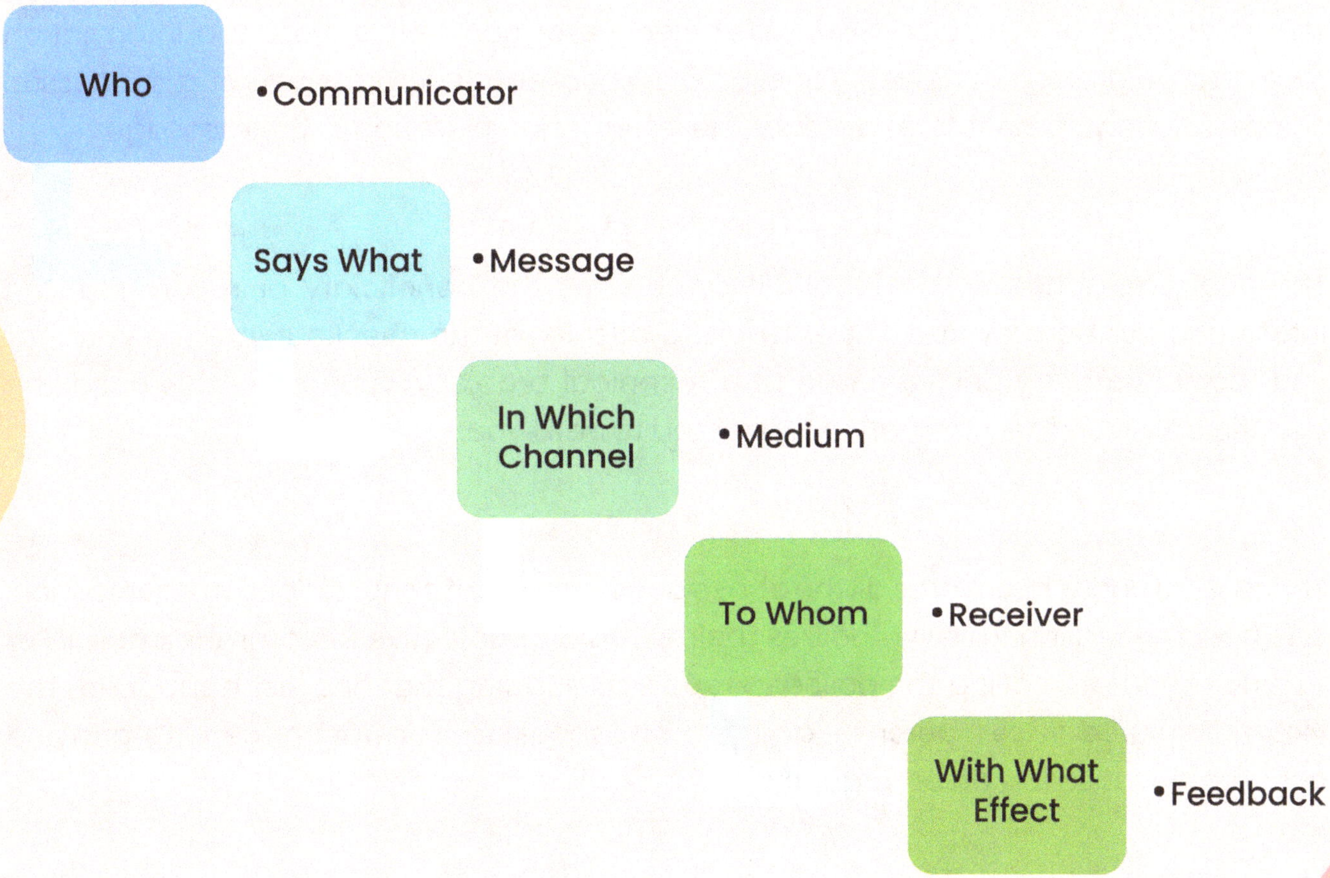

| Who | •Communicator |
| Says What | •Message |
| In Which Channel | •Medium |
| To Whom | •Receiver |
| With What Effect | •Feedback |

### 3.1 Who: The Entity/Person

This component refers to the communicator. The person who starts or creates the message. This first component symbolizes the source of the message. For example, if your friend says hello to a group of friends, some might hear it, while others may not, and they will ask who said it. After you brief them, they will recognize where the message came from.

### 3.2 Where: The Medium

This component symbolizes the area, place, device, communication tool or region in which the message is being exchanged. The medium can be of many types, from physical places to transmission devices. For example, an announcer in Times Square, New York, is telling about tonight's curfew timings; the medium is the speaker device.

### 3.3 What: The Object

This is the actual message, the main objective of communication. The information that is to be given or received. For example, a colleague informs you of a successful shipment of equipment from abroad. The information of import is the message.

### 3.4 Whom: The Collector

The final component in the chain. It symbolizes the beneficiary or receiver of the information to be provided. For example, a cashier at the checkout informs you that your card has been declined due to a technical problem. You are, in this case, the beneficiary since the information is directed toward you.

### 3.5 Why: The Essence

This last component governs all the above ones in terms of context. For communication, one needs a reason. This symbolizes the reason and objective of communicating. For example, you are calling the police to report a mugging that has just happened. The victim is injured in self-defense, and you are speaking at a fast pace with growing concern because it is an emergency.

# Chapter 4:
## Communication Enhancing Activities

Communication is an essential key. This book is about to develop your communication skills by honing your social skills. Both communication and socialization are interlinked. By creating a positive consequence in one, you create a positive effect on the other. This is a vital piece of information for you to know before starting this chapter and reading through its activities. For teenagers, it is very important to create effective communication skills because these skills will help them not only in their teenage years but also in their adult life. There are many communication-enhancing activities, but I will only discuss the ones fit for teenagers, ones they can understand and do.

In the previous chapter, we discussed in detail about communication, its significance, modes, importance and implementation. This chapter will inform you about some of the many social activities that build and improve communication specifically. Let us dig in!

## 4.1 Explore New Customs & Cultures

Exploration never ends! Especially in the current age where you can sit at home and easily learn about and connect with others from across the globe. Learning and reviewing new cultures, customs and norms are very good for kick-starting your social system. There are many ways to get into a new culture; learn the language, delve into the food and cuisines, participate in celebrations and cultural festivals, and talk to a friend of a different background about their upbringing and experiences.

Think of culture as a sort of medium or gateway to understanding its group of people. For example, colorful, traditionally designed clothing and spicy food are signature acknowledged customs of Indian/Pakistani culture to the world. Getting to know new cultures can help you to be knowledgeable of the diversity around you. It will aid you in interacting with people of different identities and backgrounds. To know and communicate with a person, you must first understand their roots first. So, learning new cultures helps your social and communication skills.

## 4.2 Help People

The most common and effective way of enhancing your communication skills is to interact randomly with people with or without intent. This includes helping people at any given moment. When you help someone, you give yourself a chance to develop your socializing ability and improve your communication skills.

Your parents must have taught you ever since you were a kid that helping others is kindness, and yes, it most definitely is! I believe in doing the kindness of helping others. You, in this way, help yourself and bestow some kindness on yourself too. For example, if you help an elderly person with a task, they will always bestow blessings on you, and you grow to have more respect for that person in the long run.

In this case, when you help someone, you interact with them, listen to them carefully, and put your mind to thinking about a solution. You then respond to the person and communicate with them through your verbal language and body language. This act of helping improves your communication skills.

## 4.3 Join Clubs/ Societies

You can join a wide variety of various kinds of clubs and societies for improving your social connectivity. You may join a chess club, a group for those who are interested in real crime and listen to the top podcasts for teenagers, or even a gaming clan; there are so many options!

Check to see if there is a recreation book for your community or a site that includes all of the various clubs and associations available to join in your area. The advantage of being a member of a club is that you have the opportunity to select the kind of organization that best suits your needs in terms of the amount of connection and socialization you wish to gain from the experience.

I remember my time in college. Back then, I used to actively work in the fine arts society. It was so fun and engaging. I learned a lot about the world through art and also made many friends. Since there was a constant state of interaction with the other members, I developed communication, specifically to communicate effectively with the art community.

## 4.4 Discussing Topics Randomly

This activity is equally beneficial for parents as it is for their teenage kids. Now, you may feel, what should I talk about? How will the other person react? This is normal to think, especially for anxious teens, but do not hesitate.

Encourage yourself to bring up a conversation about anything; the news, current affairs, asking about someone's day, their interests, their dislikes, their thoughts on certain matters, anything. This will help you in many ways; it will enhance your ability to act spontaneously and react logically, it will build your confidence to speak on matters of all kinds, will strengthen your speech skills, polish your body language and build your overall social skills.

Speaking up on different topics with different people helps you to increase your knowledge. It can also clear your misconceptions and mistakes, enhance and improve existing knowledge of a topic, give you the freedom to have and say opinions about that topic while listening to others' opinions and thoughts and give you a chance to process all that information and socialize with the other person accordingly. With time, after frequent practicing and discussions, you will learn and adapt yourself while communicating during a discussion or an argument.

## 4.5 Charades

Charades is a game in which teens are given a clue and then mime to help participants predict what the clue is. In order to participate in this game, you will first need to split the group into two teams, and then you will need to come up with clues based on things like book, movie or song titles. Instruct your friends to choose a clue one at a time and then gesture the clue to their team. The team should then guess the clue within a time limit of 45 seconds. If they are unable to correctly guess the clue within the allotted

amount of time, the opposing team should be given the opportunity to do so.

This allows you to practice your nonverbal communication skills while also providing you with an opportunity to exercise those skills. Teenagers learn emotion regulation, which is crucial for developing positive connections and expressing themselves effectively through role-playing and visual depictions of emotional expressions and reactions in social skills activities.

# Chapter 5:
## Activities to Boost Confidence and Manage Shyness

Confidence can be safely stated as a medium or vehicle for socialization. More than half of a teenager's communication relies heavily on their ability to speak, act and express themselves without hesitation or fear. After all, what is knowledge without efficient delivery? So, listen up well, kids! You must be confident in what you say or do, or however, you socialize with other people, because a strong personality is mostly complemented by a long-lasting impression. Such an impression can be created for other people only if you present yourself and your perspective with sheer confidence and determination without any hint of uncertainty or hesitation.

Seeing the current social state of the world, there is a dire need of firm and enhanced confidence building and training among teenagers. Some teens are naturally shy, and some are forced to be shy as a result of societal pressure. Either way, feeling shy is normal and somewhat acceptable, but it should not be at all, be a constant part of a teenager's psyche or personality. With the activities described in this chapter, I aim to rid you of your shyness and strengthen your confidence.

## 5.1 Start Small

Exercising social behaviors such as eye contact, confident body posture, introductions, small conversation, putting up questions, and get-togethers with the individuals you feel the most comfortable around is a great way to improve these skills. Smile; everyone likes seeing a happy person. Increase your self-assurance by doing so. After that, try doing it with some fresh faces in your social circle.

Consider some topics that could be used to start a conversation. Starting a conversation with a new person is frequently the most challenging aspect of doing so. Consider ways to start a discussion, such as by introducing yourself to the other person. It is much simpler to approach someone when you are prepared with a discussion point (or several of them). Starting small is the initial landmark for every kind of teenager to start interacting with new people individually or as a team.

## 5.2 Board Games

Playing indoor games is a great way for shy teenagers to start their social skill development. Since many indoor games require a small number of players, generally around three to six, this allows teenage players, especially shy ones, to begin communication at the beginner level instead of rushing through a crowd and becoming anxious.

The vast majority of retailers selling board games also regularly hold game nights or, at the very least, encourage customers to play games in the store at any time. A board game pub is a great place to meet fresh faces with similar interests and spend some time enjoying a shared pastime. Ludo, Uno, Chess, Scrabble etc., are examples of many such interactive games.

For those who are more reserved in social situations, role-playing games like Dungeons & Dragons and similar RPGs can be a fun way to get to know others while also enjoying the freedom to role-play and act as a persona of their own conception.

## 5.3 Rehearse What You Say

When you are prepared to attempt something that you have been ignoring because of your shyness, such as making a phone call or having a conversation, mark down what you intend to say beforehand so that you do not forget it. Practice saying it out loud, and consider doing it in front of a mirror. Do that immediately, then. It is okay to worry if it is not exactly as you have been practicing it or if it is not flawless. Some of the things that people who appear to have more confidence do are perfect, though. You should feel proud of yourself for giving it a shot. When you will attempt again, it will be even better since you will have figured out a simpler way to do it.

This helps to prepare not just shy teens but also confident teens when they feel down, or their confidence gets shaken at times, so rehearsing what you ought to say or do before interacting with someone, creates good social skills, boosts confidence and omits any errors beforehand.

## 5.4 Practice Being Assertive

Since shy people can be too concerned with the reactions of other people, they tend to avoid situations in which they might cause disruption.

That in no way indicates that they are weak or timid by any means. However, this may indicate that they are less prone to assert themselves. To be assertive means to take a stand for yourself when you should, to ask for what you desire or require or to tell other people when they are stomping on your toes. When you ask for what you want or need, you are being assertive.

This activity is also helpful for confident teens who may have difficulty enforcing their opinion or idea to a willing audience. Being assertive can be thought of as a necessary evil sometimes to get your social interaction going.

## 5.5 Uncover Abilities

Teenagers of today are less likely to engage in extracurricular activities than their predecessors, but a teen who develops a passion for anything will never be bored, and that passion may even persist into adulthood. Inspire yourself to try new things. Sewing, robot-making, and woodworking are just a few examples of creative hobbies. Taking

up such hobbies can help you to learn. How? You will communicate and socialize with mentors and experts to learn the ability and, therefore, will always stay in interaction with them on a constant basis, thus nourishing your social skills.

Teenagers can talk to people who they feel close to or trust the most. Consulting with trusted people and trying out various extracurricular activities can guide teens to unlock a hidden talent or ability. This newfound revelation can be a turning moment in the teen's life or reality. Such abilities and talents can further help you in making important life decisions. In the long run, if one actively participates in these activities, they learn socializing, communicating and interacting with other members of the same group and can further grow their already-skilled ability.

*Reveal Hidden Talents & Abilities to Build Self-Confidence*

# Chapter 6:

## Activities to Build New Relationships and Friendships

Creation and destruction are both equally existing parts of the natural world that we live in. In the same way, building new relationships while losing a few ones in life is normal. How is it that one forms new social relationships while losing a few from before? The answer to this question lies entirely in the concept of socialization and communication. It is through adequate socialization that we build new relationships with people or lose people as a result of defective communication and socialization. My advice for you teenagers is, to always be the better person and spread positivity amongst your social group.

The activities in this chapter will discuss in detail how you can push your boundaries and create and foster relationships and friendships amongst new and existing social circles. While there are many activities that can help you widen your social circle, I have written down some of the most important ones which I believe will help you most.

You should keep in mind that as a teenager, your social circle is still developing. As you grow and become an adult, it becomes more permanent over time. So the point is that you should always beware of who to trust and befriend, and this is something you would have to judge or figure out on your own intelligence.

### 6.1 Get a Part-Time Job

There are many positive outcomes when youth takes on part-time work. A job can provide you with financial independence while also providing valuable lessons in responsibility, teamwork, and more. Having a job also gives a teen the chance to mature and get ready for the world beyond high school. A part-time job enables teens to expand their social circle, hence allowing them to enhance their social skills on a broader range. Not only that, but teenagers also learn how to socialize in a professional circle as opposed to socializing in a personal circle. They learn the differences between both and also adapt to communicating with each person respectively.

## 6.2 Volunteering

Teens can find a variety of volunteer activities year-round. Many of them don't even call for a dedicated time slot on a consistent basis. Some examples of teen volunteerism include reading to younger patrons at a library, strolling dogs at an animal shelter, and producing vegetables to donate to a local soup kitchen.

Kids of all ages can benefit from volunteer work. Involve your teen in volunteer work at places like hospitals, animal shelters, and retirement communities. Volunteering to read to or instruct younger children is another option. Parents must assist their teens in realizing how they may aid their community by organizing volunteer efforts. When the adolescent helps others, he grows in his interpersonal abilities.

Volunteering is a very liberating activity. It allows a teen to get out of their comfort zone and gives them an opportunity to be more practical and vocal. This opens them up to being more communicative and social with unknown people and familiar acquaintances, both.

## 6.3 Do Theater

Teenagers can broaden their social circles and learn about various cultures through theatre. Inquire with community theaters in your area to see if they are accepting new young actors. Meeting other people in the theatre industry could be a great way to expand your network of creative people, allowing you to develop your own unique artistic voice. Young people who don't thrive in the spotlight may want to look into the costume or production departments at local theaters.

Doing theater also helps you understand and connect with the character. I believe for someone to resonate or relate with a character is a sort of communication because not only do you capture the physicality and appearance of the character, but you also absorb their personality traits and emotions into yourself as well. In this way, you practice socialization the same way your character would do. For example, if your character is a motivational speaker, you can connect with the character on how they communicate with a large audience.

## 6.4 Summer Camps

Teens would benefit enormously from attending summer camps that offer a wide variety of entertaining activities. Find a summer program that is suitable for you. Camps are fantastic environments to meet new people, engage in conversation with total strangers, and collaborate on projects with them. Teens who are lacking in social skills can benefit tremendously from participating in day or weekend camps. Even introvert teens can benefit from meeting new people and participating in a variety of activities by acquiring the skills necessary for appropriate social interactions. There is a wide variety of content available for summer camps, including artistic and athletic pursuits, as well as academic subjects.

Other than participating in camps as a student or learner, if you are a teen with experience in coaching and managing extracurricular events, you can join camps as a teacher or a coach and instruct other teens or younger children through the activities being held at the camp.

## 6.5 Interact with Pets

Nature is a great means of communication, not only with other beings but also taking a deep look into oneself. I believe socialization does not just come from human beings around us but also from non-human living beings too. This includes animals, birds, and even reptiles and fish. Now, communicating with animals is obviously not the same as with humans.

Communicating and socializing with animals rely heavily on cues, body language, and symbolism. You must be thinking; why is it essential to interact with animals when we are talking about social development for a teenager? The answer to this is simple. Humans are not the only living beings blessed with the natural gift of socialization and communication. Since ancient times till this day, humans have actively interacted with animal-kind and have successfully gained from it as well.

Aside from this, interacting with animals is therapeutic. You can understand their emotions by reading their gestures and relating them with their voices. Teens can join various training programs for pets such as cats, dogs and parrots. Think of this activity as a small helping hand for the more advanced real-life socialization with people. This activity is excellent for animal-loving teens.

*Interacting with Pets Comes with a Lot of Social Benefits*

# Chapter 7:

## Other Activities to Polish Social Skills

This chapter has many miscellaneous activities that will help in developing practical social skills in teens including a vast array of versatile activities. While reading this chapter, you may stop at the titles of some activities and think about how these are even considered activities as you are viewing the conventional idea of activities in your mind. It is necessary to understand that an act that you do that is rewarding and benefits you in a certain way can be termed as an activity in general.

### 7.1 Indulge in Sports

Everyone from the highly skilled to those who simply want to get out of the house and have some fun can find a place in one of the many sports leagues available in every metropolis and even many smaller communities. Active people can join soccer leagues, while those who would instead relax while staying physically active can play a round of golf.

There is a good reason why sports have such a significant weight in one's life. People can get a great deal of knowledge through participating in sports in addition to the fun value. Through participation in sports, adolescents can gain an appreciation for the value of support, cooperation, organization, leadership, motivation, and fitness. All of these traits are wonderful for developing one's character as well as boosting one's ability to interact with others.

## 7.2 Dancing

You might be thinking, how is dancing an activity that builds communication and socialization? You would be surprised to know how this actually helps to build social skills in teens. For teens who wish to take up dancing classes, they will be in constant interaction with their instructors from the dance class. It ensures a daily dose of verbal interaction by learning through words, lyrics, music and non-verbal techniques by practicing the actual dance moves in front of the mirror and assessment from the instructor. You will learn to be more confident in your speech and body.

This activity is especially significant when you plan to perform as a group. The ability to coordinate and balance your body and movements with fellow performers on stage or in practice is helpful for body mapping or body control.

Dancing might seem like an unconventional activity at the start when it comes to developing social skills but I highly suggest you give it a try before thinking otherwise and don't miss out on this opportunity.

## 7.3 Martial Arts

Some kids find great benefit from participating in martial arts like karate and others. Discipline, strength, flexibility, and agility are developed, and a sense of honor, hard work, and respect are instilled via participation in the sport. Self-defense is often included in these programs as a means of bolstering students' morale. However, some moms and dads may wonder if their kids will learn violence through karate and be concerned about possible physical harm.

When deciding to enroll your teen in martial arts courses or not, there are a number of factors to think about. Find out what to expect from each program and how to evaluate them to pick the one that's best for your kid. People of many ages, races, and walks of life can find common ground and form lasting bonds through their shared interest in martial arts. Joining a martial arts school can provide you with a sense of community with people who share your interests and aspirations.

If your child has a hard time relating to others at school, a martial arts program may provide a welcome distraction. For kids who have gone through anything traumatic, this can be a great benefit. When students bully one another or when introverts have extreme anxiety in group settings. A new beginning represents a clean slate. A class can be an excellent place for new friendships to take root.

Furthermore, martial arts teach both self-assurance and self-control. Kids who struggle socially, often also struggle to control their emotions and actions at the moment. The practice of martial arts is predicated on the idea that it will help one to become more self-controlled and thoughtful. When applied to children, martial arts training has been shown to reduce disruptive, impulsive behaviors.

## 7.4 Horse Riding

A great outdoor activity for teens who enjoy traveling on short journeys. In horse riding, teens who love animals, especially equines (horses, donkeys, ponies etc.), can enjoy creating a bond between the horse and themselves.

It's important to remember that riding horses is about more than just the attachment that forms between a youngster and their mount; it also involves social interaction that follows with becoming a member of a club or taking riding classes with other people. Aside from school and their specific social context, it gives you a chance to meet and engage with people from a variety of backgrounds, which paves the way for building connections with one another that are founded on a shared passion for and comprehension of horses.

## 7.5 Skateboarding

Skateboarding is not only a sport but also a form of art and a culture. It also fosters friendships between individuals who come from a variety of diverse social and cultural backgrounds. Skateboarding is quickly becoming one of the most popular activities

that people all over the world participate in together. It is believed that there are more than 100 million active skaters today. In spite of what the majority of people and parents believe, skateboarding does, in fact, offer some incredible advantages for both the mind and the body. These advantages are independent of the fabulous clothes, shoes, and attitude that skateboarders are known to wear. One of the most wonderful aspects of this activity is that it may be carried out in a variety of environments, including inside, outdoors, in open or closed places, and even in cramped quarters.

In fact, skateboarding is a great way to meet new people. Spending time with a group of people who share a passion is a ton of fun. Plus, there is a community of skaters willing to offer tips, tricks, and assistance to anyone who needs it. You can figure out how to talk to people and create friends. Skateboarding is a terrific pastime for shy kids to get out and meet new people.

## 7.6 Video Gaming

A fun method to encourage your teenagers to interact with other people and open up to them is to host a game night at a party or during a family function. Asking participants to think of their own games to play during these kinds of activities can make them more exciting. Vote on the submissions to choose which ones are the greatest, and then have a good time. You will develop superior socialization skills as a result of the bonding experience.

In today's world, playing video games together can be a fun way to make new friends. Even the least appealing games will have online communities that are active, and the more famous ones will have massive online communities that you may join. The formation of a gaming club is an excellent approach to bringing together a small group of individuals to play with and become acquainted with.

There are also events that take place in real life for video games, such as tournaments, online multiplayer and other get-togethers. These are typically focused on playing games on personal computers, but there is also a sizable community for playing Smash Bros. and other console games.

## 7.7 Join a Team

The development of social skills should always include learning how to collaborate well with others. Mentors can provide their students the opportunity to address problems

and contribute to a broader goal by organizing a project of community service for a group of teenagers.

Share some examples of service projects with your teenagers, such as a weekly soup kitchen or a nonprofit talent show, and then offer your guidance and assistance while they organize their own initiative over a few weeks.

### 7.8 Go on Tours

Taking a tour of a museum, historical place, nature park, or any other form of tour can be a pleasant way to get out of your home, and you can primarily select how much you wish to engage with the other people on tour. You can choose to simply follow along and listen, or you can ask questions and become more active in the experience.

It truly depends on the time of year and where you are located as to whether or not there are tours of Christmas lights in your area over the winter holidays or whether or not there are tours of scary house decorations around Halloween.

### 7.9 Go on Long Drives

One of the many expressions of teenagers is freedom. Many teenagers in their prime age love to go on outings for long periods of time. This is a good activity as you can learn much about the world when on the road rather than at home from behind a screen because it gives you a more practical approach to interact with the world and society. Going on long drives does not only mean that you just drive and drive and drive. No way!

Obviously, you require breaks once in a while to refresh yourself at pit stops and cafes. Teens on long drives can learn to socialize with the world and people on their own terms in a range of their personal freedom. This also lets teens develop stronger personal relationships with fellow travelers when they communicate individually or as a group.

## 7.10 Try Puzzles

While most puzzles are more of a single-player mode, there are also many puzzles that permit multiplayer and teaming up. In the process of putting together a puzzle, teens set and achieve manageable goals, which can only boost their sense of accomplishment and confidence. A teen's boosted self-esteem is excellent, and they are better equipped to face future obstacles if they are able to complete a task that initially seems impossible to them, which can also be incorporated into their social skill development.

Puzzles help with development in numerous ways, including social ones. Teenagers' cooperative play is enriched and encouraged by puzzles because they require teens to work together to achieve a common objective. Studies have also shown that children's brain development is significantly affected by their ability to actively engage with and shape their environment. The prominent examples of puzzles are the Jigsaw puzzle and scrabble.

## 7.11 Get Out!

Famous all over the world, Escape Rooms are also known as Escape Games. You can get one almost anywhere, and its popularity is rising. The uniqueness of these life-size games is a significant element of their appeal around the world. While many people have probably experienced a classic Escape Room by now, others may be hesitant to do so due to concerns about large groups or a lack of funds.

However, teens should definitely try these escape rooms. Think of them as a realistic simulation of action-adventure or horror video games. When you enter an escape room with your teammates, it is your objective to "escape." Think of the room or the situation in it as a puzzle.

You are strongly encouraged to engage in conversation with the people around you in order to successfully navigate difficult circumstances. Teams are put in a position in which effective communication is required when participating in escape rooms. As your lives become increasingly entwined with the digital world, the act of physically conversing with one another may, in the future, become extinct. Escape games, on the other hand, reawaken a dormant need within people to confer about potential solutions and conquer obstacles as part of a group.

## 7.12 Collective Gardening

Collective gardening is effective in a manner distinct from those of other activities designed to build social skills because it teaches adolescents how to care for a living thing.

Gardening with other people helps you become more socially competent since it forces you to take care of things and teaches you responsibility; you simply can't ignore your plants. Teenagers may find it easier to relax after participating in this activity because it generally takes place outdoors.

### 7.13 Watch Movies

An all-time favorite social activity for teens living in the modern age. Teens love to be entertained. So why not make use of an entertainment activity as a means of learning social values as well? After all, you are not going to stay a teen forever, so you might as well enjoy movies and make use of them in a technical way while you are at it.

It is always fun to watch movies together. You and your friends can get to learn a lot about the world and how things work in the world, about people through cinema art and visual storytelling. How can you gain social skills through movie watching? The explanation for that is relatively easy. You or your fellow movie-watchers will be curious to know the plot, twists, suspense etc., and you will discuss it with each other. This conversation about the movie will spark creative thinking, listening and speaking opportunities.

### 7.14 Learning Music or Instruments

Once a teen has mastered the fundamentals of a musical instrument, he or she can join a band or other musical group, which is a fantastic way to stay social and engaged with others who have a similar passion for music. Attempting to learn a musical instrument is a very private and independent activity for teenagers.

You will need to put in the preliminary work of learning the instrument, which can take about a few months to a few decades before you are at a point where you will be capable of collaborating with other musicians at a similar skill level; however, the harder you work, the sooner you will be able to make that happen.

### 7.15 Singing

In the previous activity, you learned how to develop social skills with fellow singers and musicians by learning and rehearsing songs with your peers. Teen social and emotional growth is greatly aided when they share in musical activities like singing together. Because of the shared experience of singing in a chorus, children can develop a healthy regard for one another's unique qualities and find a sense of community.

Increased feelings of belonging in one's community A strong sense of social belonging, of a sense of belonging to our group, is substantially connected with singing skills. Group singing improves our ability to connect emotionally with others. Singing together, whether in a choir or a small group, has many mental, emotional, and physiological benefits.

### 7.16 Join a Book Club

While reading the book, most of the time is spent by yourself, hence a book club may be a great social activity for those who are a tad more introverted. This is because there are only occasional meetings in which everyone gets together in person.

It is a fantastic way to include some concentrated social connections into your life, and there are also book clubs that actually happen entirely online, so it is an excellent way to do so without having to make a significant dedication other than the amount of time it takes to complete the reading. When it comes time for everyone to gather together and talk about it, you are free to disclose a lot or as little as you choose after that.

## 7.17 Arts & Crafts

Through participation in art classes, you can not only develop your artistic potential but also see an improvement in your ability to interact with others. You will not only have the opportunity to engage in conversation with the teachers and other pupils, but will also have the chance to express your creative side. Children who have trouble speaking their minds often benefit from participating in this exercise. In order to get their feet wet, you should encourage your teenagers to sign up for any artwork or craft class they can find. Teenagers are able to better communicate themselves to others by participating in hobbies such as sketching, painting workshops, fabric art, ceramics, sculpture, and other similar activities.

## 7.18 Bonfire

You should plan some campfire evenings for your friends and cousins. You should organize gatherings where your extended family may spend time together, either so that they can be better acquainted with one another or to reflect on happier times in the past. You should inspire your teenager friends to organize a birthday party that is distinct from the norm and include a night around a bonfire as the stunning backdrop for having fun with your pals.

Bonfires are a great way to experience fun and entertainment through a great opportunity for socialization. It builds your communication skills as you get to meet new people and socialize with them over discussions, activities or events planned at the bonfire night.

## 7.19 Parties

Hanging out with your friends on all kinds of parties your parents and guardians allow you to can be very exciting, fun and a chance to learn many things. Parties are quite a common gathering event in today's world. Some examples include dinner parties, birthdays, weddings, auctions, clubs etc. A party is a social event to commemorate positivity, it calls for celebration and revival. Teens can benefit immensely by interacting with many different kinds of people.

## 7.20 Informative Trips

Set aside time to engage in socially beneficial pursuits. You should travel to the nearby towns and check out the museums there. Teens who are interested in learning more about the past often visit bookstores to peruse the wide selection of books available. Parents of teens should look into lectures and seminars given by subject matter experts, and either tag along or offer to foot the bill if their teen wants to attend with a friend.

Teens can learn a lot about themselves and the world around them on educational travels, and they can also meet plenty of new people. A timid child may need a lot of courage only to pose a query during the Q&A portion of a lecture. Assist them in breaking the ice and starting a conversation with the museum guide or even a complete stranger.

## 7.21 Live Events

An adolescent might have a life-changing experience by going to see a live performance with their family or with their friends. Live events such as championship sports, dance performances, music concerts, quiz shows, competitions, and other similar events can be viewed by teenagers in an environment that encourages social interaction. They would be in the center of a crowd, the vast majority of which would be made up of unknown individuals. The adolescents will be better able to let go and enjoy themselves while rooting for their favorite team; thanks to this.

## 7.22 Discussion and Arguments

Teens can improve their ability to control their feelings and find constructive ways to express themselves by engaging in healthy arguments. You can practice talking through problems without becoming angry or attacking the other person. Those who are able to engage in an argument while still listening to their opponent are more likely to succeed as academic and professional leaders.

Having teens argue for and against opposing viewpoints on a topic helps them develop the perspective-taking ability essential to developing empathy for others. Youngsters can hone their communication, listening, and turn-taking abilities through these interactions. Different perspectives, debates, and the development of critical thinking skills have all been shown to aid in the growth of perspective-taking.

### 7.23 Critique: The Art of Perspective

For most people in the current era, the literal meaning or definition of critique is merely perceived as an act of pointing out mistakes, shortcomings, and negative aspects etc., when analyzing a specific material or idea. This is not all true! To critique means to take a detailed, deep and careful analysis of a subject matter. This involves drawing a balanced conclusion. This would require a teen to take considerations from a neutral and honest standpoint, not involving most of their personal feelings but rather previous knowledge regarding the subject matter.

Learning to critique, is a really great activity for teens. It allows them to combine creative thinking with socialization because learning critique is not something a teen can learn on their own in a few days. It requires one to study from sources, people and their experiences, and books etc., and to practice how to give their response in a written or verbal manner by combining their personal experience of the subject matter as well. So, teens, be careful with making only a logical, rational critique of subject matters so that your words and thoughts do not unintentionally ruin someone or their life.

Critiquing is all about perspectives, so have good and rational perspectives for the world to have.

### 7.24 Delve into Shopping

Shopping is a great social activity for teen girls, but teen boys are no exception too. All teens are driven and curious in their life and feel appealing new things, food, brands, accessories etc. a great thing to buy and learn about. Shopping involves a lot of socialization with your friends and family members. As you communicate with the other people around you and the staff, you gain more confidence in conversation skills and polish your body language. Teens can learn much about the world and how to interact with people on their own terms if given some freedom to go shopping on their own, having the choice to choose and buy from their own choices.

### 7.25 Dramatics & Acting

When you perform acting and dramatics for the sake of fun with your fellow teenagers, you are providing them with an opportunity to practice their social skills through the use of expressions. You can learn what specific expressions mean and identify them when other people use them in real-life discussions if you mimic your own expressions and act as though you are saying them. When adolescents who struggle with social skills learn to interpret the expressions on others' faces, it helps them feel more at ease in circumstances that include other people.

In most cases, adolescents will conceive of a situation in which they will act as if they are another person or thing. They could, for instance, play house and act out the roles of the parents, or they could pretend to be a physician, a veterinarian, a teacher, or a cashier. They are able to test their social abilities in a variety of settings thanks to each of these opportunities.

For example, when they act out the role of a parent to another child, they should learn to identify and react to various feelings, learn to diffuse potentially dangerous situations and adjust to changing circumstances.

### 7.26 Build a Virtual World

Websites geared for teens that encourage socializing and fun include multiplayer platforms on which users can build their own worlds. Teens benefit from the opportunity provided by games to consider an entire community, establish limits, and guard those boundaries. Select a game platform that you can play online and build the world you want to live in. Invite some friends to join your realm, and make sure they know the ground rules. Interact with your pals, and when necessary, be strict with the regulations.

Considering the increasingly digitalizing world, I think it is a great way for teens to communicate with each other from a vast virtual space since it connects from across the globe in an instant.

## 7.27 Nonverbal Telephone Communication

This new take on the classic game Telephone provides students in middle school with an opportunity to develop their skills in both verbal and nonverbal communication. This is also a fantastic practice for improving attentiveness, so it serves a dual purpose. This game is best played with a smaller number of people, but if you want to make it more like charades, you can play it with only two people.

## 7.28 Yoga Class

There are many positive effects of yoga, including enhanced flexibility, strength, and coordination, which can be enjoyed by people of all ages. Do you realize that it can also influence their emotional and social growth?

Breathing techniques and basic meditation form the basis of yoga, which also includes a number of physical postures. Even while it has grown hugely popular among adults, it is also thought to be a beneficial habit for teens. Increased strength, flexibility and coordination are just some of the physical benefits that students can reap from practicing yoga.

Adolescents are particularly vulnerable to bullying, low self-esteem, and social pressure during this formative stage in their lives. A foundational tenet of yoga is a commitment to non-judgment, which naturally fosters a warm and welcoming community. Yoga also enhances your sense of oneness with your physical self. Connection is the key to being accepted. A flawless physical appearance does not exist. Mindfulness, on the other hand, encourages you to value your individuality and skillset. Check out these three stances that are proven to raise your sense of self-worth and confidence.

## 7.29 Join a Gym

The adolescent years are notoriously difficult. Teenagers struggle with their bodies developing, taking on more responsibilities, and a variety of other social factors that can be stressful. Teenagers should make it a priority to engage in regular physical activity, whether it takes the form of joining a sports club or team at school, going on outings with friends such as hikes or bike rides to going full-time to a gym.

The management of stress levels, the processing of difficult emotions, and the development of leadership skills and empathy are merely four of the many social benefits that children receive from participating in sports and other forms of physical activity. In addition to helping young adults stay healthy and maintain a healthy weight, exercise also helps adolescents to manage their stress levels. These benefits have the potential to have a substantial effect on the well-being, happiness, and future prospects of a teen.

### 7.30 Start a Niche Club

Many important aspects of social development, such as openness to new experiences, tolerance of diversity, teamwork, and communication, can be fostered through a teen club's formation. All of these are valuable abilities that teenagers will need in the workforce. Pick a specific field of study in which you have expertise, experience, or enthusiasm. It may be anything from vintage anime animations to mermaid-themed novels to humorous needlepoint.

*If you want to work in a group, you can do it either in person or virtually.*

Outline the steps you'll take to form the group, including how you'll contact members and invite them to join, where you'll have meetings, and the topics you intend to cover. Create a group manifesto and code of conduct to guarantee the safety of all participants. Your social club can be formed, or its members can simply discuss their future plans.

## 7.31 Showing Empathy

Empathy is the emotional capacity to understand another person's perspective, provide emotional support, refrain from making value judgments, and ultimately spread the profoundly healing message that one is not alone. Empathy is the affinity to put yourself in another person's shoes and experience what they are experiencing. Doing this motivate you to show empathy and consider how you might help them.

The ability to empathize with others is the foundation for developing other interpersonal abilities. It aids in empathizing, connection, understanding, compassion, social competence, and the cultivation of long-lasting friendships and romantic partnerships.

## 7.32 Try a Different Career Option

For teens, it is a time of life when there is a lot of confusion and concern over future choices and career options. Today, many teens have the free choice of selecting a career of their interest. There are others who still face many problems regarding free choice. Some teens are the victims of uncertainty; they are unsure which career to move ahead with, even with freedom from their home, which is surprisingly a lot more common these days.

Such dilemmas can be a source of depression or anxiety for teens with career choice problems. I advise such teens to connect with online career counselors or career advisors from their local area or if your school has hired one. These people are professionally trained to guide teens to easily and efficiently transit into an independent, practical life.

Teens can get a variety of social skills, from speech skills, confidence and professional body language to general information regarding different careers. Changing careers can also shift or alter your social circle, which can prove to be beneficial. For example, if the social circle from your previous profession was unaccepting and uptight, it can help to change your career into one having a more accepting and friendly environment.

## 7.33 Proper Use of Social Media

There are multiple ways to use social media, especially for teens of today's world, where every teen is on social media platforms and actively using them. While I personally believe that social media does not contribute much to a teen's social skill development directly, it cannot be disregarded that social media does play an additive or accessory effect on a teen's already social skills.

Teens should be encouraged to text and call their friends or close family members from across the globe. The function of video calling allows for a more enriching experience of communication. Teens who work or are more career-oriented can use social media outside of personal reasons. They can use platforms for advertising, and marketing, distribute their projects and take up consultation work. Social media offers freedom and variety, which makes for its lack of traditional connection.

## 7.34 Commence a Project or Campaign

A significant characteristic of teen angst is acceptance or need for approval, especially in teens with social anxiety. While this may not be common, it is, however, generally observed. I highly encourage all teens to create something new and original and market or distribute it. It allows for an influx of social opportunities.

Starting a project or campaign might be rocky in the beginning. It is sometimes difficult to attract an audience but stay patient and have faith in yourself, be consistent and stay on the right track. If your original idea is not relatable to a wide range of people, it may be suitable for just a few people, and that is your target audience, and over time more people of the same mindset will approach you as your idea is further marketed. By interacting with clients and interested people on a regular basis, answering queries, solving complaints and ensuring customer satisfaction, a teenager will be learning many socialization and communication techniques.

## 7.35 Learn Self-Defense

Learning how to defend yourself can equip you to deal with various forms of violence. Being able to safeguard yourself from the common forms of abuse seen in daily life is also part of self-defense. Training in martial arts raises one's level of consciousness on how to avoid danger, defend oneself, and strike back.

Learning to defend yourself is a great way to work on your interpersonal skills. A comparison can be made between martial arts and self-defense. Being obedient to one's elders, respecting one's peers, and being tolerant of differences are all lessons fostered by this practice. As a result, if you work on improving your social skills, you'll see an improvement in your outlook. It also aids in restoring calm and equilibrium to your mental state.

*Communication & Self-Defense Go Hand in Hand*

## 7.36 Acknowledge Your Weaknesses and Failures

This may not seem like a direct social activity, but it can be thought of as a great catalyst for polishing social activities. Teens mess up most stuff more than they can get it right, which is fine! They are still learning, and making mistakes is part of that journey.

What matters is that you should take a step back and reflect on yourself, take some time to go through your actions and sayings in a day and people's reactions and consequences. If anything went south because of you, be sure to correct that. It is mostly due to miscommunication and inefficient social standing between people that misunderstandings take place.

## 7.37 Educating Yourself About Love Life and Dating

Teenage is the middle stage between childhood and adulthood. It is inevitable for teens to grow physically and emotionally into maturity, no matter how much some teens hesitate out of shyness to talk about it. I highly encourage teens not to be shy and be open to discussing adulthood-related topics with their parents, guardians or older friends or cousins.

This will allow teens to discuss concepts and problems related to their biology and psychology more openly with experienced people and, learn more and omit any

misconceptions. Discussing love, dating, emotional health, mental healing, or sexual health with your parents or other experienced people is a good social activity for teens who have plans to settle or date in the future once they come of age.

### 7.38 Handle Situations & Resolve Matters

The principle of this activity lies in bravery and confidence building. Teens should encourage and persuade themselves to be more open to leading situations. Many events and programs require leadership and initialization. Teens can make use of such opportunities and take a faithful leap into willfully taking charge of situations.

Being the leading or managing person in events and programs can be a gateway to many social and communication advantages. It can boost self-confidence and independency in teens. It will give them ways to live and navigate through professional circles and different kinds of people.

### 7.39 Do Comedic Stuff

Some teens might think "What?" after seeing the title of this activity. I know, trying something fun that can be so childish at the same time might seem silly but comedic activities for teens are not the same as kids.

A more mature sense of humor is ideal for teens. It contains a good blend of sarcasm, dark humor, roasting and many other forms of comedy. For teens with a good sense of humor and an interest in comedic entertainment, this is a great activity. You can go with your friends to live stand-up comedies or, better, perform. Theater, and dramatics clubs etc., are great ways of doing comedy. Social skills, including; self-confidence, speech, conversation, expressions, and gestures, are greatly influenced by comedic stuff.

It also helps teens with sensitive mental health issues find an escape and feel less overwhelmed by their conditions.

## 7.40 Setting Boundaries

*Are all boundaries set to impose restrictions? Do these boundaries halt socialization?*

I believe not. Some restrictions are actually necessary tools for development. Every teen should make them. It is equally necessary that you understand the context or meaning of boundaries first. For most people, setting boundaries can mean not letting other people in, which in some cases, is true. In fact, the actual reason for making boundaries is for yourself. This is especially important for teens with anxiety. Allowing yourself to not be overwhelmed by pressures from the world is a right and duty of teens.

Setting boundaries may not directly enhance social skills or play a major role in actively developing them but it will increase your social standing and connection with people you are already social with. This can be, in a way, thought of as a passive activity.

### 7.41 Confiding in Someone

Secrets may be hidden communication entities, but they are as much part of actual socialization as any other aspect. This activity may not be a conventional exercise, but it is great for shy and anxious teens to build self-confidence, empathy, and trust with close people or even new people that you feel comfortable with. Confiding in someone can provide you with reliability as a person. This builds confidence and trust, which creates a better connection allowing you to openly and freely express yourself to familiar faces and then to more people with time.

### 7.42 Be an Apprentice

To learn is to interact, and to interact is to socialize. In ancient times apprenticeship was quite commonly practiced and well respected. Adolescents can start learning a specific profession or skill from a master and adopt them as a profession for their entire lives. Who knows, it may serve as your side business in future.

Even though the modern age does not view this culture as a notable norm, it is, however, very much present. A teen can take up any hobby, skillset or pre-career development opportunity and learn and work under the supervision of an experienced senior figure or instructor. This activity can help teens develop strong, long-term bonds, self-esteem, empathy, and understanding, which can be very good for their social skills.

### 7.43 Learn from Around You

Teens are not so highly perceptive as adults as they are still developing mature traits. As teens, you can use your five senses combined with uninterrupted focus to catch on happenings and incidents happening around you. This is more of an indirect social activity for humans. You have the capacity to learn and adapt to your environment by observing people talking, their body language and seeing their gestures. You can benefit heavily from it.

### 7.44 Go On Short, Spontaneous Hangouts

Sudden meetups, out of random are a great way to boost your social skills too. A surprise event out of pure randomness can engage teens and drive their instincts and social, mental and emotional factors.

### 7.45 Role-Play

Somewhat similar to theater and acting. Role-play games and activities have many positive effects on the social life of teens. Any teen can be anyone at any time. They can act or imagine scenarios, characters and stories with fellow teens or by themselves. It will drive a sense of knowing one's place in the community as a teen.

*Role-Play as A Social Activity*

# Purpose

Final thoughts and closing argument are that youngsters who are entering adolescence should make the world their training ground and center stage. This will nourish you with experience and personality building opportunities.

I sincerely hope you will make good use of this book and actually implement the social activities in your practical life too. Social skills building is very important as it shapes you up to the person you will become in the future.

Learning socialization and communication is something innate and some must be learned from the world through experiences and encounters. Knowing who you are to your core depth as a person and acting with the world accordingly using your principles is crucial in learning about communication abilities both theoretically and practically.

In this book, there are many activities that cannot be categorized as actual activities, but their working principle and benefits are all the same.

*Hope to see you as a social pro someday!*